WHAT'S INSIDE A
Toaster?

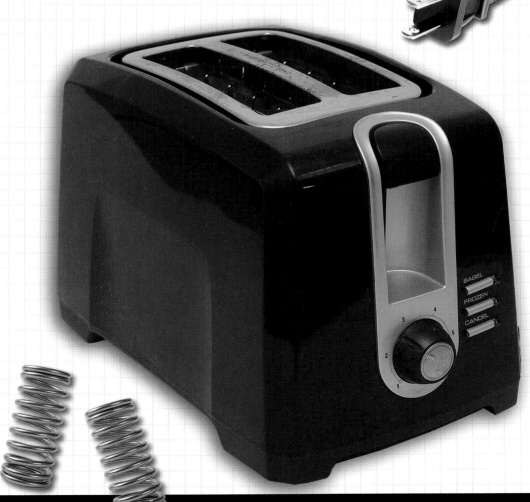

ARNOLD RINGSTAD

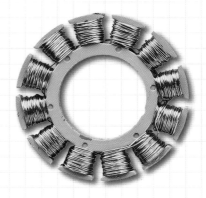

Published by The Child's World®
1980 Lookout Drive • Mankato, MN 56003-1705
800-599-READ • www.childsworld.com

Photographs ©: Rick Orndorf, cover (toaster), 1 (toaster), 4, 6 (crumb tray), 7, 9, 11 (top), 11 (bottom), 13 (top), 13 (bottom), 14, 15 (electromagnet), 16, 17, 19 (dial), 20 (crumb tray), 24; Shutterstock Images, cover (spring), cover (plug), 1 (spring), 1 (plug), 2, 3 (circuit board), 3 (plug), 5 (glasses), 5 (scissors), 6 (wires), 8 (screw), 10 (wires), 10 (circuit board), 12, 15 (circuit board), 18 (spring), 18 (wires), 19 (toaster), 21 (springs), 21 (wires), 22, 23; Praiwun Thungsarn/Shutterstock Images, 3 (screwdriver), 5 (screwdriver), 8 (screwdriver), 20 (screwdriver); Shyripa Alexandr/Shutterstock Images, 5 (gloves)

ISBN 9781503832084
LCCN 2018962813

Printed in the United States of America
PA02419

About the Author

Arnold Ringstad lives in Minnesota. He enjoys making toast with peanut butter and cinnamon.

Contents

Materials and Safety

Materials

- ☐ Phillips screwdriver
- ☐ Safety glasses
- ☐ Scissors
- ☐ Toaster
- ☐ Work gloves

Safety

- Unplug the toaster, and then cut the power cord before taking it apart. Throw the end of the cord away.

- Always be careful with sharp objects such as screwdrivers.

- Wear work gloves to protect your hands from sharp edges.

- Wear safety glasses in case pieces snap off.

Toaster

Phillips screwdriver

Work gloves

Scissors

Safety glasses

Inside a Toaster

Toasters heat up bread. They make it crispy. The heated bread is called toast. People spread butter, jelly, or other things on toast. Then they enjoy it for breakfast. How does a toaster work? What's inside?

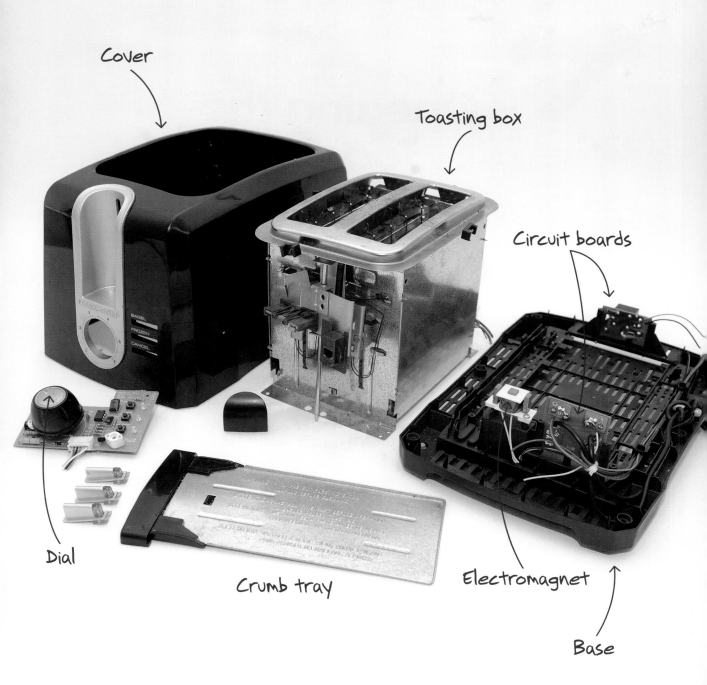

Cover

Toasting box

Circuit boards

Dial

Crumb tray

Electromagnet

Base

Opening the Toaster

Several screws hold the toaster cover and base together. Find them in the bottom of the base. Then unscrew them. Once the screws are out, you can pull the cover off. You may have to remove the **lever**.

Safety Note

The screwdriver is sharp, so be careful when removing the screws.

Inside is a metal box. You will also see **circuit boards** and wires.

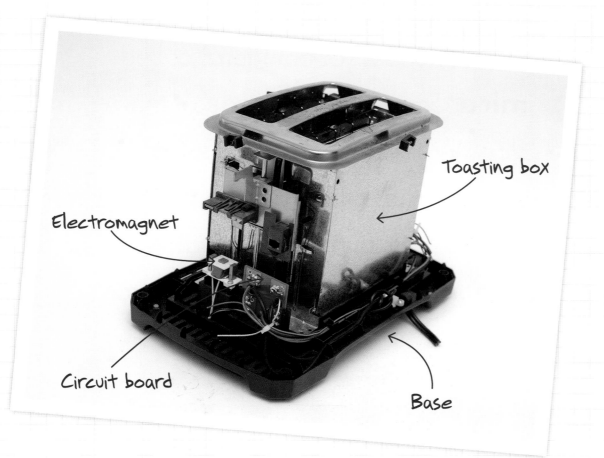

Electromagnet

Toasting box

Circuit board

Base

The Toasting Box

The metal toasting box holds the bread. It has two slots. Inside the box are sheets of a mineral called **mica**. They face the inside of the slots. Wires run across the mica sheets. The bread rests in metal cages. It sits on a small metal platform. The bread does not touch the wires.

Mica sheets

Wires

Metal platform

The Lever
and Spring

The outside of the metal box has a lever and a spring. They are connected to the metal platforms inside. Pushing the lever down lowers the platform. This lowers the bread into the toaster. The spring pulls the lever back up. It raises the bread back up again.

When the lever is up, the spring is at rest.

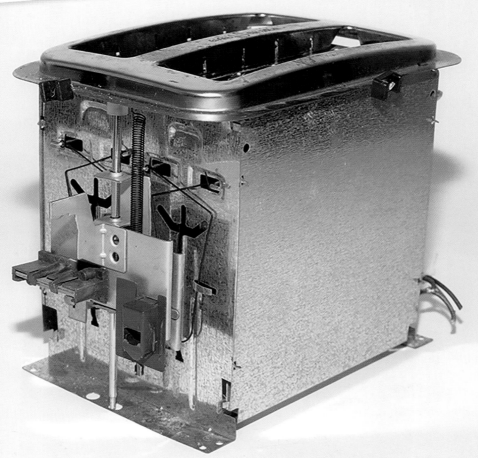

When the lever is pulled down, the spring stretches out.

Magnet Power

Electricity comes into the toaster and goes to a circuit board. This circuit board has two separate pieces of metal on it.

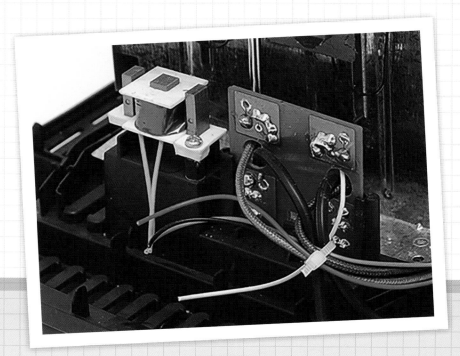

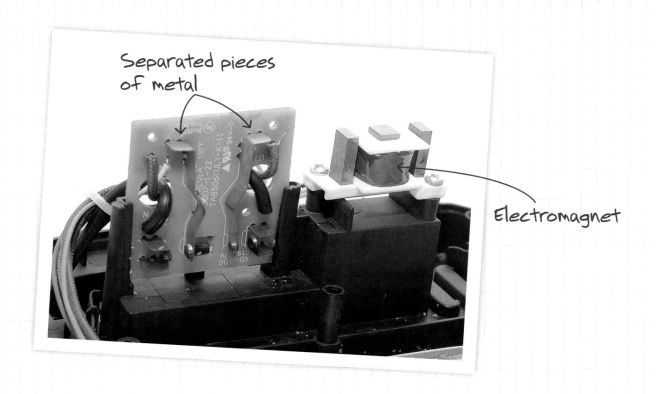

Separated pieces of metal

Electromagnet

Pushing the lever down connects the pieces and lets electricity flow. This powers the **electromagnet**, which then holds the lever down while bread is toasting.

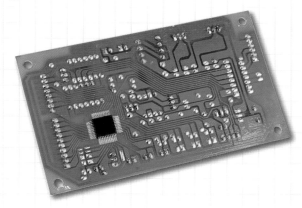

Heating Up

At the same time, electricity flows to the metal box. It goes through the wires and heats them up. This makes the inside of the box very hot. The metal cage protects the bread from getting too hot. The bread darkens. It dries out and hardens. A tray below the box collects any stray crumbs.

Wires carry electricity into the metal toasting box.

Time to Eat!

The **dial** on the front tells the toaster how long to heat the bread. A longer time means darker, crispier toast. The circuit board can tell where the dial is set. It stops the flow of electricity at the right time. The electromagnet turns off. The spring pulls the toast up. Now the toast is ready to eat!

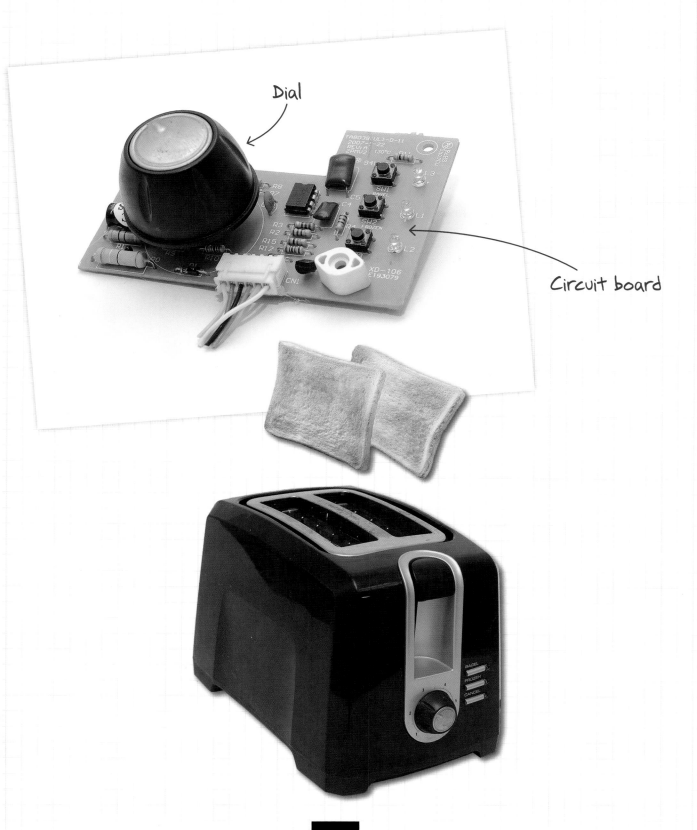

Dial

Circuit board

Reusing a Toaster

We've taken apart a toaster and learned what's inside. Now what? Here are some ideas for how to reuse the parts of a toaster. Can you think of any more?

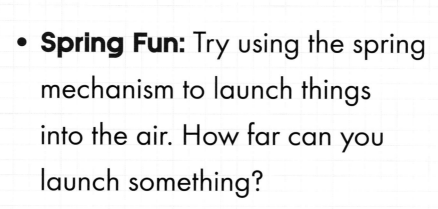

- **Spring Fun:** Try using the spring mechanism to launch things into the air. How far can you launch something?

- **Wire Bracelet:** The toaster has many colorful wires inside. Try cutting out a few to create a multicolored bracelet!

Glossary

circuit boards (SUR-kit BORDZ): Circuit boards are pieces of material that hold computer chips, switches, and other parts. Inside the toaster, circuit boards connect to the dial and send power to different parts of the toaster.

dial (DYE-uhl): A dial is something that a person spins in order to use a device. On the toaster, a person can spin a dial to choose how long to heat the bread.

electromagnet (i-lek-troh-MAG-nit): An electromagnet is a magnet that only pulls things toward it when electricity flows through it. Inside the toaster, the electromagnet holds the lever down while the bread is heating.

lever (LEV-ur): A lever is a handle that you move to use a machine. The toaster has a lever that you push down to lower the bread into the toaster and start the heating process.

mica (MY-kuh): Mica is a mineral that blocks electricity and can stand up to high heat. In a toaster, mica sheets hold the hot wires.

To Learn More

IN THE LIBRARY

Fisher, Valorie. *Now You Know How It Works.*
New York, NY: Scholastic, 2018.

Holzweiss, Kristina. *Amazing Makerspace DIY with Electricity.* New York, NY: Scholastic, 2018.

Ringstad, Arnold. *What's Inside a Radio?*
Mankato, MN: The Child's World, 2020.

ON THE WEB

Visit our website for links about taking apart a toaster: **childsworld.com/links**

Note to Parents, Teachers, and Librarians: We routinely verify our Web links to make sure they are safe and active sites. So encourage your readers to check them out!

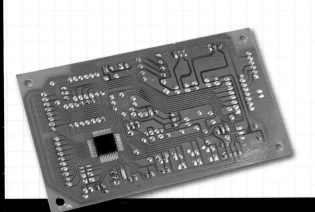

Index